Lights, Camera, Action!!

A Beginner's Guide to Overcome Camera Shyness, Record Videos, And Build a Digital Presence

– ARMANITALKS

Table Of Content

Introduction

Welcome to Lights, Camera, Action!! This is a beginner's book which is going to teach you how to speak in front of one of the finest pieces of technology out there, the camera.

My name is Arman Chowdhury, the founder of ArmaniTalks. A media company which helps engineers and entrepreneurs improve their communication skills so they can express their ideas with clarity and confidence.

For the past couple of years, I've been growing one aspect of the ArmaniTalks Brand which is extremely important for this book, the YouTube channel.

Within this YouTube channel, I've posted over 300 plus videos, have done a dozen plus interviews, and I've worked with different entrepreneurs in helping them launch their YouTube channel so they can take their ideas from their mind to the outside world.

This book is going to focus on a lot of the high-level principles regarding speaking in front of the camera. We're not going to go too much in detail or discuss too much about the technical setup.

Instead, we're going to be tackling the beast from head on.

We're going to be talking about:

- Why camera shyness is a thing in the first place.
- The nitty gritty fundamentals of putting in the work and understanding that everything is a

muscle, even building comfort in front of the camera.

- How to understand our ideas, clarify it, and create it.
- The art of hitting that publish button so **at least** one person can see our work.

Let's get started with lesson number one.

Part 1:

Shy?

Why Camera Shyness Exists

Glossophobia, do you know what that means?

It means the fear of public speaking.

Cynophobia, do you know what that means?

It's a fear of dogs.

I don't know the name of the phobia for the camera, but I know that camera shyness is a thing.

There are plenty of people who will avoid events that requires them to speak in front of the camera because they're too nervous.

I want you to understand that camera shyness is completely normal. It's unusual if you don't have it. Because here's the thing....

This technology that we have in the present-day world, the camera, is relatively new.

When someone is telling you that they don't have camera shyness or they've never had it, understand that they're very similar to the guy who knows how to walk, but as a baby, they were struggling.

They were crawling, trying to get up, they fell, they were trying to get up, they crawled some. Eventually, they learned how to walk.

As a grownup, we don't remember our struggles as a baby.

So, when you see someone that's poised while speaking in front of the camera, maybe they don't remember the beginning of their journey, sort of like that baby.

Why Camera Shyness is Normal

When you're thinking about communication, you want to view it in a very targeted manner. There are five different levels of communication:

- Level one is known as intrapersonal communication, which is self-awareness.
- Level two is known as one to one communication, also known as conversation.
- Level three is many to many communication, also known as teamwork.
- Level four is known as one to many, which is public speaking.
- And level five communication is human to machine, also known as media.

We're predominantly focusing on level five communication for this book. Level five is new in terms of history.

So, let's get imagine that a ruler represents the entire civilization that ever existed. If we're trying to assess how long speaking to the camera has been a thing, it's a millimeter of that ruler. You can barely see it.

Which shows that speaking in front of this inanimate object is new. Anytime we're doing something new, there's discomfort.

I'm bringing all this up because you want to have the right expectations from the get-go. When you understand that this journey is supposed to be difficult, you can approach this skillset with the right mindset.

Speaking in front of an inanimate object is never supposed to be simple, and that's why overcoming camera shyness is **huge**. You're going to have a brilliant skillset for this generation and in the next section I'm going to be talking about the value of learning the skillset in the first place.

Importance of Speaking on Camera

YouTube channel, Zoom meetings, saying a toast which is going to be recorded at a wedding... Three simple situations of when you may be expected to speak in front of the camera.

If you know that the recording light will not fluster you...

Then you have an edge in this world.

Nowadays, the era that we're living in is known as the information age, where global communications is bigger than ever. It's easy for someone from the US to speak to someone from Italy as though they were next door neighbors. A lot of the communication is going digital.

If you are one of those rare few who doesn't shy away from digital communication, then you're going to be able to thrive in the information age.

Part 2:

Practice

Practice is the Only Way

Repetition, repetition, repetition.

Do you want to know the biggest difference between a growth mindset and a fixed mindset? The growth mindset views everything as a muscle. If they're physically capable of learning it, now it's a game of the mind. When it's a game of the mind, it becomes a game of the heart.

It's desire.

Do you want it or not?

The fixed mindset is going to mail it in, but the growth mindset is going to put in those repetitions, repetitions, repetitions.

You may have not wanted to hear that. A part of you may have thought that this book was going to be giving you the latest hacks to shortcut the process.

No, it doesn't work like that.

Every single person that learned how to speak in front of the camera had to first navigate through the discomfort stage.

They got up, fell, got up again, and repeated that process in iterations.

Just know that we're going to be stressing practice throughout this book, but more importantly, we're going to learn **how** to practice.

Dark Zone vs Light Zone

I want to introduce a new concept called the dark zone versus the light zone.

The dark zone is all the videos that you record in private.

To this day, I have hundreds of videos in my laptop and camera that I never plan to release. These videos are just for me, so I can experiment with ideas, understand where I stand on certain issues, and experiment.

It feels good when you have a certain zone that you know no one is going to judge you for. This is known as the dark zone, **your zone.**

The light zone is the public space.

This is when you are allowing other people to see your ideas, watch your videos, and every now and then... give constructive criticism.

> **What I recommend is that we start off with the dark zone and then we transition smoothly into the light zone.**

The more that we focus on the dark zone, the more that we start to improve our body language, understand our ideas, and create unique insights that you're not going to find on any search engine.

Let's take the dark zone very seriously.

So, we make a smooth transition to the light.

Private YouTube Channel

I wish someone told me what I'm about to tell you right now. There have been plenty of videos that I've recorded on my phone and on my laptop, but one of the best areas in order to create your dark zone is YouTube.

Now wait, before you panic about everyone watching your videos, did you know that you could make your YouTube videos private before you decide to ever make it public?

There are plenty of videos on my YouTube channel that I keep private to watch for myself.

The reason that I like YouTube is because you may have hardware issues with your laptop and even with your phone. Be serious. How often do you have the same phone now that you had two years ago?

Rarely.

But with YouTube, the beautiful part is that once you upload the videos, you can access it from any part of the world as long as you have an internet connection. When you have this channel, you're capable of watching your growth in real time.

Watching your growth in real time is similar to a man who's been struggling with obesity for a long period of time, and he finally decided to get a good gym instructor. This gym instructor is different. Sure, he's making this obese man go to the gym, eat right, sleep well.

But he's also making this person take progress pics.

As this obese man sees his progress pics, he feels more motivated to keep shedding the pounds. There's a feedback loop that builds incentive to keep moving forward with the journey.

That's the same exact thing with the YouTube channel, the private one.

So, start a YouTube channel, start uploading some videos on there, and make it private. This is going to be your dark zone.

Publish Videos

You don't want to be that guy who is getting stuck in the dark zone, just posting videos in private all the time, never allowing other people to see it.

Eventually, you want to get to a state where you're sending your private videos to at least one person so they can see it for themselves. Or you just make it public and allow a whole bunch of other people to see it.

This may sting.

You may be thinking:

'What if they don't like it? What if they just criticize me?'

Perfectly fine. All great content creators know something. With attention, 3 groups form:

- One group loves them.
- Another group is neutral.
- And the third group despises them.

Want to know the cheat code?

View all three as the exact same.

Don't say:

'I like the nice people more than the neutral people and the neutral people more than the mean people.'

You don't want to do that.

Just say:

'All opinions are whatever, because ultimately, I'm creating for me first. I understand that this is a skillset that is going to benefit my life.'

If you let the good opinions get to your head, then the mean opinions will get to your heart.

Have the right attitude regarding the light zone. There are billions of people on this planet. There are millions of people that want to start a channel. And there are only a handful of people who actually end up doing it. But unfortunately, those handful of people are stuck in the dark zone.

Few of those individuals put themselves out there. So, when you do enter the light zone, do it with swag.

Even if you stumble, fumble, and mess up your video, just know that you're one of the rare few who have entered the light.

Part 3:

Content

What to Talk About

In the last section, we talked about the importance of learning how to practice, and we divided our practice into two different components:

- The dark zone, where we record videos in private.
- The light zone, where we make a few of our videos public.

We talked about why YouTube is an amazing resource. Mainly because you're able to watch yourself grow up in real time, and you are able to access a YouTube anytime you have an internet connection.

In this section, we're going to be talking about what to talk about. Because when the recording light is on, a lot of times, your brain is going to freeze. So, if you have some clarity regarding the subject matter, it's going to help out tremendously.

Talk About Things You Love

I have a very simple rule on what to talk about... things that you know extremely well.

Some of you guys are going to do the exact opposite. You guys are going to be doing research on research, writing notes, and giving yourself analysis paralysis.

Remember what we said earlier:

> **The most important part of this book is the repetitions.**

So, if you start off with something that you know extremely well, now it becomes much easier to put in the repetitions.

What do you like to talk about?

It could be anything. You don't want to judge yourself too much.

Let's say you're a big Harry Potter fan and you have been wondering whether JK Rowling was going to release more books in the future.

Talk about that and be creative.

Let's say you don't think she's going to release more books, then put yourself in her shoes.

- If you were JK Rowling, what are you going to do?
- Would you release more books?
- Do you have more stories to tell regarding Harry Potter?

Have fun. Make it creative because the more that you make it creative, the more that you start associating a positive feeling to speaking in front of the camera. When you can associate the right emotion regarding this act, now you're hacking the system. Now you're going to do this act long term.

Look for Patterns

Want to know one of the biggest differences between a leader and a follower?

A leader notices patterns while a follower has no clue.

What is leadership really?

Leadership is a game of the mind, power, persuasion, influence. They're all ideas. Whenever you're dealing with ideas, you're dealing with themes. Anytime that you're dealing with a theme, you're dealing with patterns.

In the last section, I talked about you creating a whole bunch of different videos regarding topics that you know very well. You're going to be stacking up all this data. As you're looking at this data, you'll come to notice that:

- A lot of them are rubbish.
- Some of them are so-and-so.
- But a few of them are gold.

The gold ideas are resonating the most with you. And whenever you find an idea that resonates with you, I want you to collect it like a Pokémon. Because the more that you keep collecting ideas that resonate with you, the more that you build your foundation regarding what you stand for. The more that you build your foundation, the more that you understand a communication skills law:

You always come number 2 to the idea.

When Barack Obama was first starting his presidency, there was a period in his career where he was getting a lot of criticism for his speech. The criticism was that he said, uh, a lot.

There was one-time David Letterman clipped a little bit of Obama's interview, a two-minute segment. During that segment, Obama said, uh, 30 plus times.

This was huge. A rookie quirk like this for a sitting president was no good at all.

Yet, by the time Barack Obama finished his career, he was seen as one of the greatest speakers of all time.

Any idea why?

It's because Barack Obama understood the communication skills law. He was to become number 2 to his idea.

Sure, Obama as a person may have said uh a lot. He may have had some limiting beliefs. He maybe didn't like his style too much. All normal as him as a person.

But he understood that any time he was speaking, he was now in a different ruleset. The ruleset regarding ideas.

> **_Idea comes number 1, and it can never come number 1 if you have no clue what you stand for._**

So, as you're creating your data points, I want you to do it with some intention. Look out for those ideas that resonate with you the most.

You feel it in your chest.

You don't need to intellectually explain it.

It's something primal.

It's as though the answers have been there all along.

Look for those ideas and keep making yourself aware, aware, aware. Now your foundations are getting **strong**.

Add Nuance to Ideas

In the last section, we talked about the importance of collecting ideas which resonate with you. But we don't want to stop there. We want to get those ideas and add layers to it.

When I was starting the ArmaniTalks YouTube channel, there was a certain period when I was curious regarding articulation skills.

What was it exactly?

Sure, I knew the definition regarding it, but what was articulating? The more that I thought about it, the more that I realized that it's pretty much a person thinking out loud.

When I had that simple framework of thinking out loud, I was able to see a stunning parallel between articulation skills and the gym.

I told you in the beginning of this book that speaking skills are a muscle, and I wasn't exaggerating. With speaking skills, we're thinking out loud and with going to the gym, we're training in the visible.

As I was starting to play with this idea of articulation skills more, eventually, I ended up creating a concept known as the Articulation Chamber.

This chamber is when you reserve a part of your home to create ideas. Sort of like how you go to the gym to strictly work out, it's the same notion strictly with articulation skills.

Notice what happened... In the initial stages, I found an idea that resonated with me, but I didn't just stop there. I started to ponder on it, dwell on it, started to add tiers to it, and that's when I was able to create a new idea:

- The Articulation Chamber.

So, the more that you are recording these videos, the more you want to keep adding nuance to past videos.

A lot of the times, you are going to surprise yourself. You are going to be thinking of innovative concepts which can provide a bunch of useful value to someone else. That's because you took the time to keep adding layers to an idea.

Part 4:
Delivery

Camera Etiquette

In the last section, we talked about what you're going to be talking about, especially when the recording light is on. It's important to start off by speaking about topics that you know well versus topics that you need to research. The main reason why is because you cheat code past analysis paralysis and start putting in your reps.

As you start putting in your reps, you're going to notice yourself collecting a whole bunch of different data, and through that data, there are going to be certain ideas which resonate with you the most. Collect those ideas, but don't just stop at collecting, add nuance to those ideas. The more that you add nuance to the ideas, the more that you're going to create new ideas in the process.

Now, as you're doing all of this, use this section to learn some basic camera etiquette. By failing to implement any of these forms of etiquette, the whole process of speaking in front of the camera is going to be filled with tension.

Let's eliminate the tension. Let's allow it to melt off. Let's make speaking in front of the camera fun and easy.

Talk to Only One Person

When speaking in front of the camera, your goal is to speak to only one person rather than a general audience.

In the beginning, it's going to feel like you're speaking to a whole bunch of different people.

But notice that anytime that people are consuming video content, they're consuming it predominantly one at a time. Even in movie theaters, sure a lot of people are watching the same movie, but they're processing it in their mind... one person at a time.

You want to train yourself to speak to one person.

Because if you're trying to speak to a whole bunch of different people, you will look all over the place with a glazed look on your face. The audience is getting a filtered version of you.

When you're only speaking to one person, everything takes care of itself. Who is this one person going to be?

Up to you.

For me, I like to envision that I'm speaking to my younger self. I know other people like to envision that they're speaking to their dog. Some people envision themselves talking to their best friend, their younger brother etc. You could get creative with it. And if you don't even want to make it too complicated, just focus on building a relationship with a camera.

Your best friend was a stranger at one point. Think about that. This friend that you have so many inside jokes with, memories with, bonds with...was a stranger.

In the beginning, you guys weren't that cool with one another. You guys needed some time.

- Time to let the guards down, build the bridges, and start planting the seeds for the jokes.

Likewise, it's going to be the same thing as you're building the relationship with the camera. Just know that you're speaking to one person, not a general audience, and this is the first etiquette that you need to imprint into your mind.

Fix Posture

- In communication, you could do a whole bunch of things wrong, but if you make the other person feel heard, they will love you.
- In digital communication, you could do a whole bunch of things wrong, but if your posture is right, then you will love the process.

In the beginning stages of recording videos, you'll notice that your posture is not the best. Especially because you're nervous.

You cannot always control the mind, but you can always control the posture.

Chest out, back straight, shoulders peeled back, chin up, and you can even do a gentle smile. By doing this, you come back into the present moment. The more that you can prime your body to have a great posture when the recording light is on, you kill two birds with one stone.

The first bird is that you improve your posture and look more presentable.

The second bird is that rather than being in your head too much, you're in the present.

Over time, these little incremental changes start to add up. So, carry yourself like the CEO of a planet.

Informal
Beats Formal

When I was younger, most of these individuals from the mainstream media were extremely formal. Very serious tone, a serious face, not too many jokes, just straight to business.

But nowadays, where more and more content exists, where more people want to build a relationship with the person's content that they're consuming, rules are changing.

> **Formal no longer wins, informal wins.**

Yes, there's a time and place. You don't want to be the guy in front of a camera who is acting like a straight up baboon. But if you're one of those people who is capable of telling jokes, use this to your advantage.

If you don't like telling jokes, then prime the mind to keep being like:

'Hey, it wouldn't hurt to tell a joke every now and then. Or, what about you smile a little so you can loosen up.'

The more that you can loosen up from your own state of being, the more that you release mirror neurons in the other person. And mirror neurons are the 10th wonder of the world, right behind Pareto principle and the compounding effect.

So, when you can feel good yourself because you are chasing informality over formality, then other people who watch your videos are going to feel good as well.

Part 5:

Refine

Importance of Watching Film

In the last section, we talked about a few basic camera etiquettes to keep in mind. Although those camera etiquettes seem small at first, the more that you're practicing, the more that you'll start to notice the effects getting bigger.

If you instill the good habits from the beginning, you'll get good fruits. If you instill the bad habits from the beginning, you know the story.

In this section, we're going to be talking about the importance of consuming your content back. I want to make this as tangible as I possibly can, so you're actually doing this rather than skipping the step.

If you watch your own content back, I guarantee you you're going to speak so much better in front of the camera. So, let's get started.

Psycho-neuromuscular Theory

Psychoneuromuscular theory.

Wait, before you run away, this theory isn't that complex. It's a theory that a lot of athletes use in order to become top performers. Floyd Mayweather is consistently watching his boxing matches back. Tom Brady is consistently watching film. Kobe Bryant? He used to watch his entire games back right after he was done playing.

The psychoneuromuscular theory states that when you're consuming your own content back, it's firing off thought waves in your mind which is influencing your nervous system to behave in a different way.

When you break it down in a very logical sort of way, you are watching **yourself** back.

This makes you question your sense of self. You're used to seeing life from a 1st person perspective. Now you are seeing yourself from a 3rd person perspective?? It's going to be extremely cringe at first to watch yourself on tape.

Push through it.

Everything is a muscle. Remember?

> *The more that you keep watching yourself, the more that you are going to notice yourself fine tuning yourself.*

Sort of like big data and artificial intelligence. Both need one another. If you try to process big data with your laptop, it's not going to work. You need complex hardware that artificial intelligence can provide. But if you just have artificial intelligence without any data, then how is it going to refine in movements?

When you combine big data with artificial intelligence, you get magic.

That's how a lot of self-driving cars work.

Similarly, when you're watching your content back... Your nervous system is the artificial intelligence and the content is the big data.

Combine the two and you slowly start to get more polished over time.

Content & Warmth

What should you look out for as you're watching your content back? You don't want to get super specific. You don't want to break down every single word, like:

'Ah dang, I should have used this word instead of this word. '

> **As you're watching your content back, you want to focus on the gestalt of things.**

Gestalt means the high-level picture.

Whenever you're watching your content back, you want to let your body do the talking. Your body is going to tell you when certain things feel right and when certain things feel off. Whenever your body is serving as a compass, listen to it. Because the more that you keep listening to your body, the more that you're going to build a genuine **feel** for the camera and the warmer your personality is going to become.

That's not to say that your body is going to be telling you everything. You still want to evaluate the content.

Is your message any good?

In the beginning stages, if you're seeing a whole bunch of random stuff that doesn't make any sense, that's fine.

You're still gathering data.

But the more that you're putting in your reps, the more polished that your message should be getting.

- Are you enjoying it?
- Are you learning from it?
- Are you being entertained by it?
- Is it providing some sort of value?

- Can it benefit at least one person if they were to watch it?

Watch your content like that.

Extra Things to Look For

Here's a few more tips to watching your content back.

The Holy Eternity:

- Facial gestures.
- Palms.
- Tonality.

If you have no clue how to read your body yet, just look out for these 3 variables.

- How is your facial gesture? Is it stiff the entire time?
- How is your tonality? Are you monotone the entire time?
- And how are your palms? Do you show your palms at all? Do you

show them a little too much? Do you point a lot?

Look out for a few of these variables.

Content wise, you just want to ask:
> ➢ Am I using 50 words when I could have used 5?

Because the purpose of clear communication is to keep our message concise. As you're watching your videos back, get a general feel for whether or not you're being efficient.

Simply bringing conscious awareness to these two different things, the Holy Trinity and excess words, will allow you to fine tune your delivery.

Part 6:

Recap

Summary

We covered a bunch of different topics in this book, so let's do a quick recap to make sure that we understand the big points.

We talked about why camera shyness is a thing in the first place. It's normal. It's normal to not want to speak in front of an inanimate object.

How are you going to speak with life to a lifeless object?

Through practice.

But you're never going to practice unless you understand the practical importance of learning how to speak in front of the camera.

A few of the practical benefits are:

- Record YouTube videos so you can scale your business.
- Get your message out there in the world so you're not running away from Zoom meetings.
- Record the video in the wedding when the bride and the groom ask you for some thoughts.

Once you understand the practical benefits, you have to practice.

There are tons of different ways to practice. But what I recommended in this book was to have a dark zone and a light zone.

Dark zone is when you are gathering data and experimenting with different ideas in private.

Light zone is when you are making your videos public.

Where are you going to create videos?

- On YouTube.

The beauty regarding YouTube is that there's a private feature that you can use anytime, and you can make your videos public anytime.

You are on the right track if you're making videos about topics that you know **very well.** You could always talk about topics that you need to do research on later in the game, but we want to avoid any form of analysis paralysis in the beginning.

Keep on recording videos, keep on stacking up your data, and eventually, you'll find certain ideas which resonate the most with you. Collect those ideas and add nuances to those ideas. That builds your foundation, so you start to build more confidence in front of the camera.

As you're building the confidence, you want to make sure you're focusing on the right etiquette.

You don't want to be speaking to 50 different people in front of the camera because you'll look like a deer stuck in the headlights. Keep it simple. Speak to one person, fix your posture, and enjoy the process.

As you're accumulating this data, you also have to watch your videos back.

Your body will tell you what to look out for, which allows you to fine tune your movements in the process. The more that you fine tune your movements in the process, the better the next video is going to become, the warmer your personality is going to become, and the more simplified your message will be.

Conclusion

Thanks for giving me your time. If you enjoyed this book and want to watch my content, you could always follow me on the ArmaniTalks YouTube channel.

Or you could just go on www.armanitalks.com where all my social media channels are comprised in one location so you can stay updated with the ArmaniTalks brand.

Thank you for joining me, and I'll catch you another time.

Think Fast

A Beginner's Guide to Impromptu Speaking, Clear Thinking, and Concentration Skills

Think Fast is a guide to learning impromptu speaking skills and improving concentration levels. This is a beginner-friendly book to turn thoughts into ideas and ideas into words. Think fast and adjust to any situation you are presented with.

In Think Fast, You Will Learn:

- The benefits of learning impromptu speaking.
- How to focus better.
- The power of daily 1% improvements.
- Frameworks on how to practice impromptu speaking.
- How to monitor your progress.
- Challenges to expect when speaking off the cuff.
- Ways to use impromptu speaking to create compelling content.
- How to link the mind, breath, and body into 1 unified system.

Scan The QR Code

Get To The Point

A Beginner's Guide to Essay Writing, Critical Thinking Skills & Logical Reasoning

---

Get to the Point is a beginner's guide on how to write essays, use critical thinking, and break down complex topics with the use of logical analysis. Essays are a profound way to build your body of work and solidify your philosophy. Learn the art and science of essay writing in this book.

In Get to the Point, you will learn:

- How to create a compelling subject for your essays.
- The use of logic, words, and critical thinking to break down complex topics.
- Effective strategies to research your topic.
- A quick way to build a to build a rough draft.
- A simple framework for editing your essays to sound more conversational.
- The art of proofreading.
- How to overcome imposter syndrome and publish your work.
- Strategic ways to grow your digital empire with the use of essays.

Scan The QR Code

Synergy

A Beginner's Guide to Negotiation Skills, Persuasion & Win-Win Deals

---

Synergy is a beginner's guide on how to negotiate better, improve your persuasion skills, and create win-win ideals. We live in an interconnected world. Graduate from competition mindset and adopt the collaboration mindset.

In Synergy, you will learn:

- Spot good deals from bad deals.
- Turn a no into a yes in the making.
- Deal with aggressive personalities.
- Confidently ask for something from others.
- Implement the synergy negotiation lifecycle to create win-win deals.
- The proper way to ask questions to extract information.
- A bonus section to build persuasion skills.

Scan The QR Code

LOL

A Beginner's Guide to Comedy, Telling Funny Jokes, and Conversational Humor

---

LOL is a beginner's guide to comedy, telling funny jokes, and learning how to incorporate humor into everyday conversations. Being funny on demand is a skill. It's a skill that allows you to disarm tense situations and spread joy.

In LOL, you will learn:

- Spot good deals from bad deals.
- Turn a no into a yes in the making.
- Deal with aggressive personalities.
- Confidently ask for something from others.
- Implement the synergy negotiation lifecycle to create win-win deals.
- The proper way to ask questions to extract information.
- A bonus section to build persuasion skills.

Scan The QR Code

9 7 9 8 8 6 8 9 7 8 2 6 5